# Super Beagle

### By Kim Edge Ambler and Rell Ambler

Published in 2018 by Peirce Street Publishing
Rhode Island

peircestreetpublishing@gmail.com
www.peircestreetpublishing.com
Copyright © Kim Edge Ambler and Rell Ambler, 2018

ISBN-13: 978-0-692-15721-3

**Many thanks to our crew!**

**From Rell:**
**This book is dedicated to:**
my family in California
my papa and grandma
my cousins
my aunts and my uncles
my dog, Angie
my mom
my dad
my sister
my friends

**From Kim:**
**This book is dedicated to:**
my daughters and husband
my mom and dad
my sister, TK, Caleb and Katelyn
my non and pop
my West Coast Ambler family

**Special shout-outs:**
**Editors:** Harold and Annalee Ambler

**Readers:** Christie and Cece Cambio,
George and Patty Edge, Michaela and Ben Kellogg,
Holly and Stella Jensen, Jenn Snively, and
Mrs. Kowal and Cavanaugh's 1st grade
Frenchtown Elementary Class 2018

**Production support:** DJ Hart and John Neilsen

**Inspiration:**
Katelyn Fitzgerald, who saved us
with her quick ideas on the color pink

To our very own Super Beagle, Angie, whose
gentle spirit, love of people, speed, and floppy
ears remind us daily that dogs are magic.

# Hello!
## My name is Blue.

My mom named me Blue, because I am a bluetick beagle. I wonder sometimes if that means I am actually the color blue?

But I don't think I'll ever know, because we dogs are all color-blind!

With a name like Blue,
it's hard not to think
about color every minute.

All I hear
during the
day is ...

"Come here, Blue!"

"Time for dinner, Blue."

"I love you, baby girl Blue."

**Just yesterday, though, my whole world changed.**

I found a mask in the woods.

When I put it on,
I could see
**ALL THE
COLORS!**

I ran so fast that I began
to fly up into the clouds.

I was Super Beagle.
And it was ...

# AWESOME!

**Dog Beach**
Santa Cruz, California

**The Chrysler Building**
New York City, New York

I flew all around the world.

I visited Santa Cruz, New York City, and Paris. Colors were everywhere, and I loved them all.

But there was one tiny problem— I didn't know which color was which. And most important, I didn't know which color was blue!

# I yelled to the sky: "I just want to see the color blue!"

**The Eiffel Tower**
Paris, France

# In a flash, the mask showed me things that were blue. Blue was so cool!

I saw the blue ocean, the blue sky, a huge blue whale, and a beautiful blue sailboat.

I learned that my cat brother, Milo,
has blue eyes and a blue cat bed.

Luckily, I speak fluent cat.
So, I heard him say:

# "Hey, Blue, I don't know my colors, either. Help a cat out!"

**And just like that Milo had a magic color mask, too.**

"We want to see red!" we yelled.

# We loved red.
# It was hot.

We took a ride in our dad's red truck. We saw his red hat, a red brick building, and a red ice cream sign.

My dad made me a very special cape
to go with my mask. I couldn't wait
to see if it helped me fly even higher.

**"Please, may I see purple?"**
**I asked as I flew up into**
**the clouds.**

**As the sun set, the world turned purple, and three purple hot air balloons filled the sky.**

I thought to myself, *I wonder what gray looks like?*

The sky and the whole town turned gray and rain clouds showered down on me from above. I liked gray because now I knew that my brother Milo was gray, but dogs do not like rain.

**So, I quickly asked.**
**"May I see green, please?"**

All the colors changed to green. My friend Hank the Turtle was all green. The grass and the leaves on the trees were all different shades of green, too. It was totally fresh! There was another color I had always wanted to see.

## "May I see yellow?" I asked.

**I looked across the street and saw Milo drinking super sour lemonade over at Leelu's Lemon Stand.**

**Everything there was yellow: the tables, the chairs, the straws, the lemons, and especially the sour lemonade.**

Milo gave me a piece of bubble gum to try and told me I should ask to see pink next.

I had a funny feeling, but I did ask!

ffffwuh

ffffwuh

ffffwuh

POP!

# Then I chewed and blew the biggest bubble that I could.

Milo was right, pink was intense. and now everywhere. I walked over to my grandparents' house to see about getting a little less pink.

I'd heard my nonnie say a million times that her favorite color was orange. So, before I opened the front door, I announced: "I want to see orange!"

**Wow! My nonnie isn't joking around about loving orange. She actually has an orange couch and orange wallpaper.**

That is one **strong** color. As I drifted off to sleep, I began to wonder about the color brown.

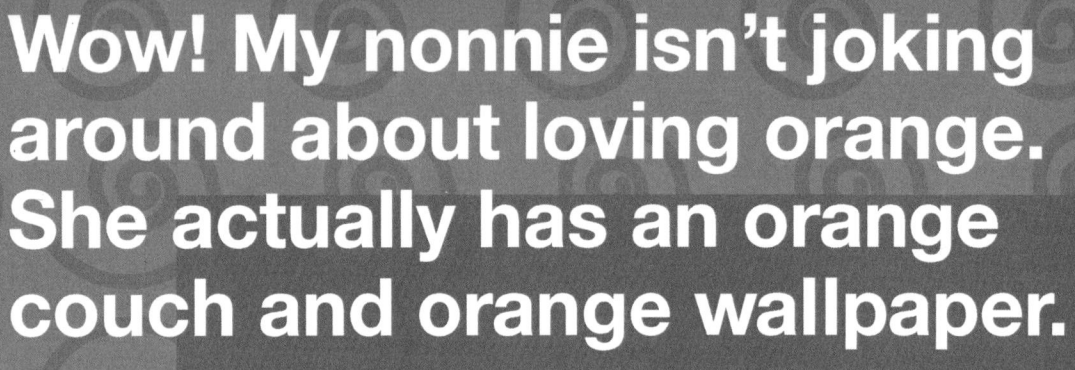

While I slept, I had a wild dream. My dog brother Boo was in it, and so was my cousin Kobe. They were both brown. They were playing brown guitars, wearing brown cowboy boots, and howling their hearts out.

## When I woke up, I had just one question left: "May I see black and white?"

Everything turned black and white, and I finally figured it out. I am not blue or red or purple or gray or green or yellow or pink or orange or brown!

I am black and white, just like a few of my very good friends.

**Lucy**
the Lemur

**Patty**
the Panda

**Sammy**
the Skunk

Everyone asks me, "Blue, what do you do when you aren't wearing your magic color mask?"

Well, I follow my nose around town, looking for kids with masks to tell me what color sweater I am wearing.

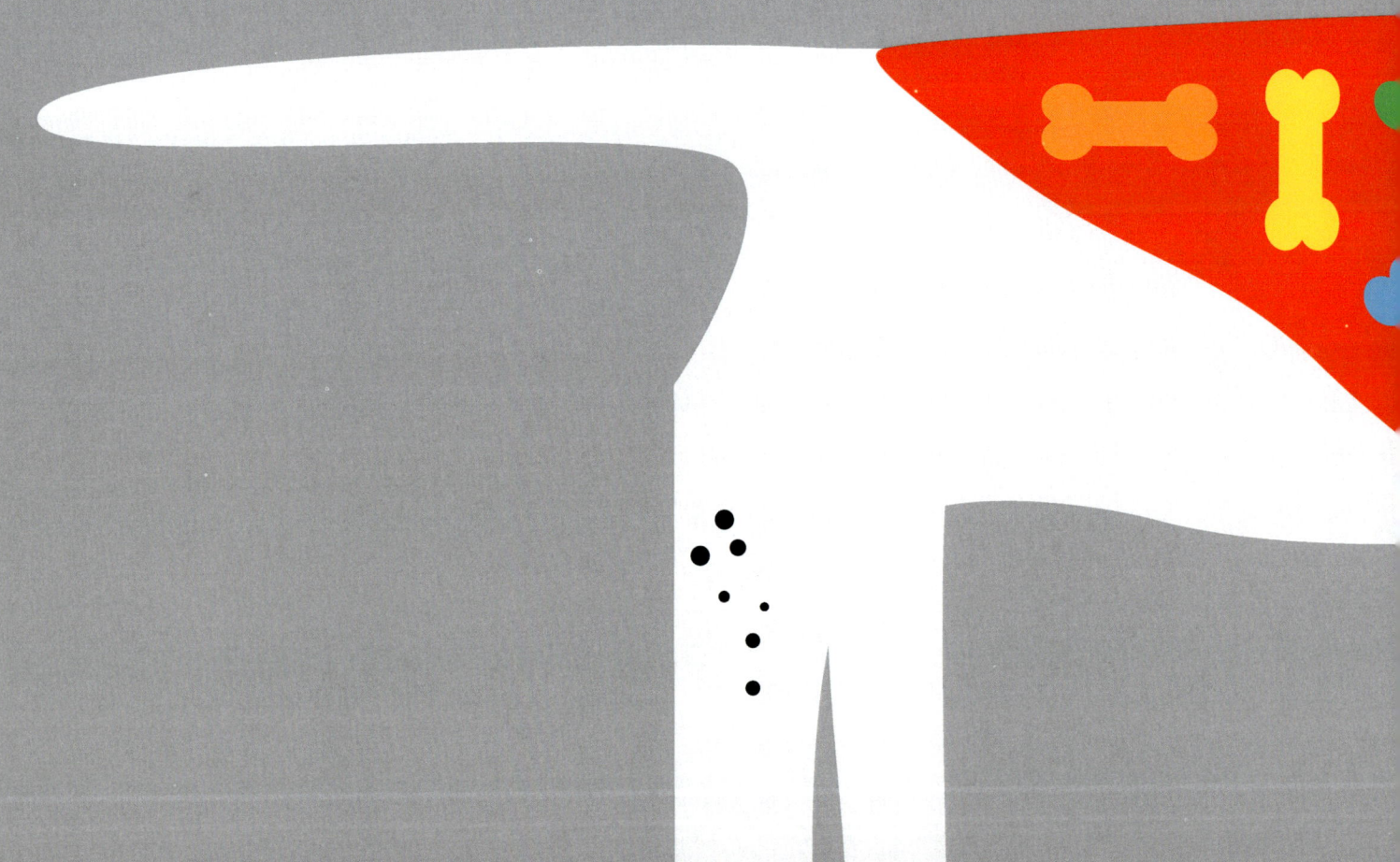

# I left you two masks of your very own.

**Will you help me figure out what color sweater I am wearing?**

**Ask an adult to help you cut these out and tie a string through the holes.**

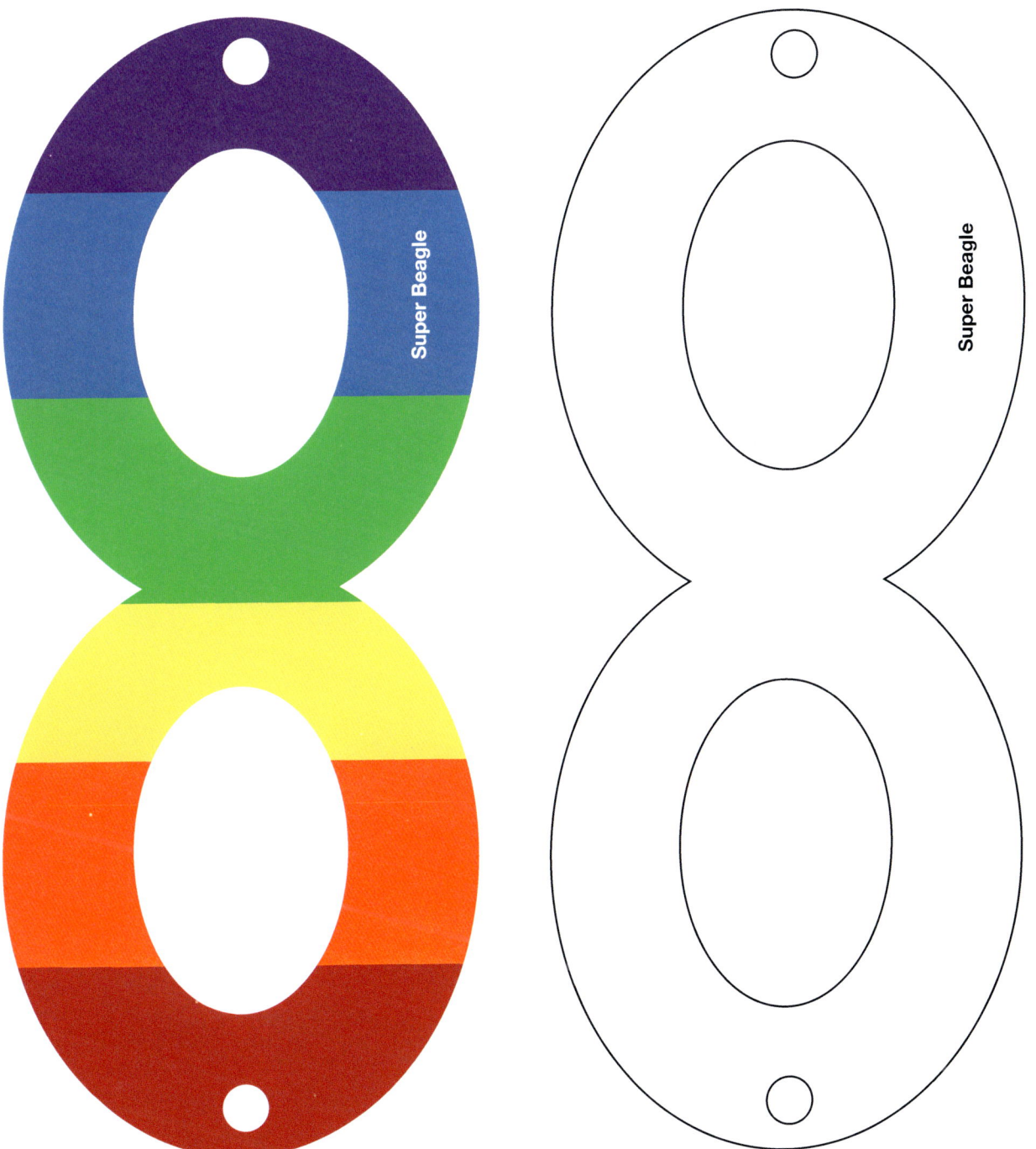

Super Beagle

Super Beagle

I can't wait to see how you color your own mask!

**These are our Super Beagle sketches.**

**This part of the book is for your Super Beagle sketches:**

Name: _____ Age: _____ Favorite Color: _____

**Follow me on Instagram:** Super_Beagle_Official
**Sketch me, share your work:** #superbeagle